Letters

CW01629729

Joan McDowell

Bracklinn Publishing

Letters of Blessing

First Published in Great Britain in 2023 by
Bracklinn Publishing, Glasgow

Copyright 2023

The moral right of the author
Joan McDowell
to be identified as the author of this work has
been asserted in accordance with the Copyright,
Design and Patents Act, 1988.

Cover Image by Sam O'Donnell

ISBN: 978-1-7395426-0-3

Dedication

This book is dedicated to Bill, my dearest and best friend.
I thank my God upon every remembrance of you.
Philippians 1.3

Acknowledgements

I am blessed to have a large family, many friends, both women and men, of all ages. I wish to acknowledge them all in this book. My life has been, and is being, enriched by the sharing of our life stories.

In writing this book, I wish to recognise the support, encouragement and guidance I received from the Renfrew Christian Writer's Group and Caroline Johnston in particular. The following were also my beta readers and provided constructive criticism: Caroline Johnston, Fiona Lindsay, Betty McKay, Jack Quinn, Lorna Smith and Joy Velykorodnyy. You are all awesome women and it has been an absolute delight getting to know you.

God bless and keep you all.

Contents **Page Number**

Introduction 1

Christian Growth 3

A new Christian 4
Choosing a new church 6
Having doubts 10
Change at church 13

Life Stages 16
Preparing for parenthood 17
First baby 21
Moving house 23
Children's choices 27
Achievements 30
Coping with teenagers 32
Going on holiday 36
Letting go of your children 39
Midlife 43
Acute ill health 47
Chronic ill health 49
Missing you 51
Growing old 53
Caring for older family members 56
Death of a parent 59
Death of a sibling 62
Facing death 65

Work 68

Choosing a career 69
Redundancy 73
Change at work 76
Not getting that job 79

Themes 82
Waiting 83
Pain 86
Be still 89
Hoping 91
Directions in life 93
Walking 97
A blessing 99

Introduction

This book is a collection of encouraging letters to support friends experiencing changes throughout life.

I have been blessed throughout my life by having a very dear family and many precious friends. These same people have encouraged me on life's journey in a variety of ways. One activity that I enjoy is that of letter writing. In these days of social media, to my mind, there is still nothing that beats the letter or card where someone has sat down and specifically written to me with a paper and pen. Over the years, I too have written many letters and cards to these same family and friends.

The thoughts from this book arose one day when someone had commented that my letter had meant a lot to them. It dawned on me that I should write a book of blessings for my family and various friends at different stages in life. This book has flowed from these thoughts.

For ease, throughout the book, the writer is a woman. In Egypt, the letter X denotes Christ. The author of the letters, although a friend, is bringing and sharing the words of Christ. The letter X also often denotes a kiss, an act of affection. It therefore seemed appropriate that each letter was completed with an X.

Also, for ease, the 'friend' being written to is a woman. The letters however may be appropriate for anyone.

There are several references in the letters to being 'salt and light' and to the potter's wheel. I believe that we are all works in progress and we will not be 'complete' until we are in Heaven. While here on earth, we are therefore constantly being refined to become more like Jesus. That process is like clay in the potter's hands and this analogy is often used within the Bible. Along the way, we are also meant to be the aroma of Christ to others, and reflect the life of Christ in all we do, and hence the references to being salt and light in our daily dealing with others.

People are invited to use these letters as inspiration or even as a template for their own writing. It can sometimes be hard to find the words to say, and so this can be considered as a resource.

All Bible verses quoted are from the King James Version of the Bible. Each verse cited, or referenced, is only used once or twice.

Christian Growth

A New Christian

O my very dear friend,

Praise God. Praise God! I am just rejoicing because He is King! I am just so very, very pleased to hear of your salvation. Our Lord is so good and so gracious. As you know, your Christian friends and I have prayed for you for many years and we are so delighted to hear that you have now accepted Christ as your Saviour. Those chains of Satan have been broken and you are now free, filled with the Holy Spirit and serving a new Master. What wonderful, wonderful news! New life indeed.

As I have prayed with you many times so I will continue to pray for you. O the joy and intimacy when we first know our Saviour, and O how quickly the devil tries to steal such joy away. You have now entered into the gates of heaven. You have now entered on the spiritual journey and spiritual battle that we are all part of. However, we are fighting with the resources of heaven and not in our own strength. We are battling against principalities and powers of darkness with the blessed blood of the Lord Jesus and our testimony.

I pray that our Lord will keep you and that nothing will separate you from His love. I pray that your love of the Lord will grow more and more as the days go by. I pray that our Lord will give you such a hunger for Him that can only be met in Bible study, prayer and the fellowship of others. I pray that the Lord shows you your gifts and talents that only He can give and that you use them for His praise and glory alone.

Truly there is rejoicing in heaven over one sinner that repents. But hey! We can also have a party here on earth when this happens.

The Lord has heard and answered our prayers. Blessed be His name. To Him be all the glory for ever and ever Amen!

Your friend,

X

1 Peter 1.8-9 Whom having not seen, ye love; in whom, though now ye see *him* not, yet believing, ye rejoice with joy unspeakable and full of glory: Receiving the end of your faith, *even* the salvation of *your* souls.

Psalm 10.16; Psalm 107.10-14; St. Luke 15.7; St. John 3.3; Acts 1.8; Romans 8.35-39; 1 Corinthians 10.31; Ephesians 6.10-12; Philippians 4.20; Revelation 12.11.

Choosing a New Church

Hi there! How are you doing in your new place? Have you found a church family yet? I know that this can be one of the hardest things to do when you move. I also know that it can be really hard finding a new church. In some ways, church is church, but, being human, we all like and, need, to belong.

I don't need to advise you to first pray about it. We both know that the Lord loves to hear and answer our prayers. He will guide you and lead you and place you where He wants you to serve Him.

I would also advise you to visit all the Churches' websites first to get a sense of what they do, what their vision is for your area and what groups there are in the Church. Nowadays it is so easy to find out such information without the embarrassment of visiting every Church and saying 'I am just visiting' when you know you are doing more than having a visit.

I wonder if you have found any other Christians yet in your neighbourhood, or at work perhaps? If you have, you could ask them about their church and listen carefully to how they describe their church family. Sometimes a local paper has a section on what churches are doing and this can be a good resource for getting a feel about each.

After doing some research, there is little to beat actually attending church. Funny how I did not recommend that in the first place, isn't it? In some ways you need to decide how important your own theology is and whether some churches are a no-go even although they appear attractive. Only you can decide what your deal breakers are and what are not.

First impressions do count, sadly. I recently attended another church for the first time and the person on the door said, 'Welcome, you are home'. I can tell you, that made me feel very welcome within my first few steps. You can fairly easily assess if a church is welcoming to the stranger as well as the long standing member. I know you can be quite shy in these situations, but please stay around after the service if tea and coffee are being served. This will give you a chance to talk with others and find out more about the community there.

Ask others about why they come to that church. I am sure people would be delighted to share this with you. It could be the friendship, the pastoral support, the young people's work, the prayer ministry, the outreach work, the worship: a whole host of things that speak of the work of the body of believers. Consider in what way does the church support the community in which it is situated. There are lots of things to find out, but all reflecting the principles practised by the early church in the book of Acts.

Belonging to a community of believers does not happen overnight and a great way to get to know others is to work alongside them. At any church you visit, have a wee look at what opportunities there are for you to serve using your own skills and abilities and not just filling a gap on someone's rota. The Church is described by Paul as being one body. All have a part. The Bible describes different gifts and talents as examples. It is not a definitive list.

Lastly, not terribly scriptural I know, but, do you feel at home there? We all have fundamental human needs of being appreciated, valued, respected, wanted and even needed. If you do not feel a welcomed part of the body, at the very beginning, then conditional love is being offered and not the outrageously generous, all-accepting, non-judgemental love that our Saviour offers.

We all have a part to play. By your very presence at church, you are contributing. You are bringing your own unique personality into the presence of God to be used by Him for His glory. You also know what your gifts are and it is important that these have an outlet within your church.

Just remember, though, that the church is the only organisation that exists for the people outside it. Also remember that, when you join a Church, you are now part of that family. To criticise it, is to criticise yourself. Think about that one.

Please do let me know how you get on. I pray specifically that you will find your spiritual home. Please call me if you wish to chat any of this through.

Much love pal,

X

1 Peter 4.10 As every man hath received the gift, *even* so minister the same one to another, as good stewards of the manifold grace of God.

Psalm 23.2-3; Psalm 133.1; St. John 3.16; St. John 15.13-14; St. John 16.13a; 1 Corinthians 12.4-10, 14, 27-28; Galatians 5.26; 1 Thessalonians 1.2; 2 Timothy 1.6;

Having Doubts

Hi dear,

I have heard that you are no longer sure about your faith and you wonder where God is and if it is all true or not. Doubts are healthy so long as they drive us to the source of our being for answers.

We are created in God's image and are emotional, physical, spiritual, social beings. How I feel one day depends as much on how much sleep I had the night before, as how my spiritual life is going. We cannot base our faith on feelings as our feelings are so contrary.

We can base our faith on facts – and the feelings will follow. As children, we sang, 'Jesus loves me this I know, for the Bible tells me so'. This is a simple fact. We probably do not need much more than that.

So, I ask you, how much are you reading your Bible? The early disciples met and read His word daily and that is a very good discipline to have. They read it daily and sometimes more than once a day. However, if you do not feed your soul on the word of God, you will soon wander and have all sorts of doubts going through your mind. There is a lot to be said for the one verse a day – on a calendar, a phone app, a promise box, that you call to mind throughout your day. There are 365 days most years, so within a year, that is 365 individual verses that have been laid up within your heart. Add to that the fact that is also good to read a passage of the Bible and follow some Bible reading notes. Dated notes keep you accountable – to yourself – and expand on the reading.

There is also a place for more in-depth study of a passage, a book, a topic and there are several resources that can support you in this.

My second question is, how much are you meeting up with your Christian family? We need each other to encourage, support and reprove one another. Iron sharpens iron. It is easy to make excuses – you are tired, you need to be up early tomorrow, it is your first night free this week. If you avoid meeting with others, you avoid meeting with the Lord in others. So, get your head and life back into gear and go! To Church, to your housegroup, your prayer group, your Christian friends. We are told not to neglect the meeting of ourselves together. Why do you think we are told that? Because the Lord knows that we need each other.

Lastly, what do you do when you have your doubts? Talk to friends or keep them in your head? Feel sorry for yourself? There is only one place that you need to go to. Take it to the Lord....which is prayer. The Lord loves to hear you talk with Him. The Lord answers your prayers even before you speak them. He loves to hear what bothers you and your doubts and concerns. I could go on and on about prayer but I will keep this short. Speak to the Lord. Only He can really answer your doubts and by the way, you know I would love to meet for coffee to talk all this through with you further. Let me know when you are free.

Love

X

Job 42.1-6; Then Job answered the Lord, and said, I know that thou canst do every *thing*, and *that* no thought can be withholden from thee. Who *is* he that hideth counsel without knowledge?' therefore have I uttered that I understood not; things too wonderful for me, which I knew not. Hear, I beseech thee, and I will speak: I will demand of thee, and declare thou unto me. I have heard of thee by the hearing of the ear: but now mine eye seeth thee. Wherefore I abhor *myself*, and repent in dust and ashes.'

Genesis 1.27; 2 Kings 19.14; Job 37.14; Psalm 19.1; Psalm 55.22; Psalm 119.11; Ecclesiastes 3.11; Isaiah 65.24; St. John 14.23; Acts 2.46; Acts 17.11; 1 Thessalonians 5.11; Hebrews 4.12; Hebrews 10.24-25; Hebrews 11.1; 1 John 4.10.

Change at Church

Dear friend,

So things are changing at church. I know that feeling well. I wonder what bothers you about these changes?

Is it personalities or people who you do not get on with, or dare I say it, you do not like, but who are now running the show and you do not like that? Take it to the Lord and may He forgive you. We are all His unique creation and His son died for us all.

Is it that you feel you have lost your position in the church family that you valued so much? In that case I need to ask, who were you serving? Yourself or the Lord? If yourself, then it is just as well that you are no longer doing that role. If you were serving the Lord, He will show you what He now has planned for you. His will – not ours.

Is it that you do not like the change? There is nothing that says that things must continue as they are. The body of people is the church and not the routines and structures and social mores. Are people still attending and coming to know the Lord? Are people growing in their faith? Are more people serving? Then be thankful that the burden is shared. It does not all depend on you but rather, it depends on the body.

The music is too loud. The music is too quiet. The hymns are too modern. We no longer sing the old hymns. There is too much clapping. There is not enough clapping. Do you know how many people have spent thousands of hours complaining about music in church worship? Have you read the psalms? Have you read Psalm 150 in particular? Do you honestly think that heaven will be quiet? We are told that there will be silence in heaven but for a specified time and a specific purpose and reason. We are encouraged to praise God with our whole beings and if that involves dance, drums and shaking the booty, I am sure the Lord does not mind! If we are gloriously in love with Him, we will lose all our inhibitions and dance before Him. King David did so – we can too.

Our world is constantly changing. There is something safe in the familiar routines. There is order, structure and safety. Maybe the Lord is taking us all out of our comfort zone to show us a new thing. To show us that it is Him we worship – our great, faithful, unchangeable God who is the same yesterday, today and forever. However, to make us more like His Son, we need to be shaken out of our safe routines. We need to learn again to trust in Him and not ourselves; we need to be hopelessly drowning in His love and let His love flow from us to others.

So things are changing at church. Go with the Spirit. Park your criticism. Stand, wait and see what the Lord is doing. We cannot go backwards. We can only go forward, with our hand in His and see what exciting things He has in store for us all.

And by the way, the Lord knows what you are thinking. He wants to take your hand and lead you gently on. Don't resist Him. Walk in tandem with Him. His yoke is easy and His burden is light when we walk with Him.

I do know how you feel. I have been there and I would not want to be there again! Go with the flow, dip your toes into the change, then your ankles, then your knees, then your whole body. You will love it!

In Christian love,

X

Isaiah 43.18-19 Remember ye not the former things, neither consider the things of old. Behold, I will do a new thing; now it shall spring forth; shall ye not know it? I will even make a way in the wilderness, *and* rivers in the desert.

Joshua 24.24; 1 Samuel 12.16; 2 Samuel 6.14-15; Psalm 62.8; Psalm 100.1-5; Psalm 103.11,12; Psalm 150.1-6; Jeremiah 17. 9-10; Lamentations 3. 22–24; Ezekiel 47.3-6; Luke 9.62; 1 Corinthians 3.4-5; 1 Corinthians 12.14; 1 Corinthians 12.27; 1 Corinthians 15.3; Galatians 5.25; Philippians 2.3-4; Philippians 3.14; Colossians 3.23; Hebrews 13. 7-8; James 4.10; 1 John 1.9; Revelation 8.1; Revelation 22.9.

Life Stages

Preparing for Parenthood

Hi my dear friend,

Thank you for opening up to me and sharing with me your deepest heart's desires. I feel privileged that you have entrusted me with this information and I am obviously praying for you and for your husband.

We are told that 'children are a gift from God' and, in that sense, they are not a right. The Lord places people in families and it is normal and usual that marriage produces children, so I hope and pray that the Lord blesses you both with a family.

So, what do we do with a gift? First, it is that, a gift: something that is given to us, not because we want it, not because we ask for it, but because the giver wants to give us the gift. So, the ability to conceive, bear and deliver a baby is all from God. If this happens to you both, it is because God wants to give you this baby. While we can follow medical advice about what assists with conception etc., ultimately, it is only God who creates new life and only He can give you this hearts' desire.

To be given a child is such a huge responsibility and privilege and fantastic fun! You will be stretched and changed beyond ways that you cannot even imagine. Life is never the same again. It is richer. It is fuller. It is trying and tiring in equal measure. You will know such a love that you would die and kill to protect your child and you never knew that you had it in you.

So how can you prepare for motherhood, if God so entrusts you with a little one? First, pray. I don't need to tell you that. The Lord encouraged us to ask, and it would be given to us. Secondly, prepare your body – look after yourself physically, mentally and spiritually. Have you any bad habits that you know you should give up? Is your physical health as good as it could be? Do you need a check up for any bits and pieces (what a hoot) that need to be sorted out? Then read. Read good books - Christian and non-Christian – on how to be a good parent. What do you need to learn? What concerns you? Talk it all through together as a couple. Prepare yourselves; it is not just about you, but you and hubby on how to parent well. Observe others in your Church. What are their parenting styles? What do you see that you think you will never do? (Please do not look at me!!!). What do you see that you would want to emulate in your family? Are there any families in your Church that you can share your thoughts with? Maybe you could ask a slightly older couple to mentor you both through all this? I am sorry that both your parents live at such a distance but do chat with them about your hopes and dreams as well.

All we really know are our own parents, for good or ill. Reflect on what their strengths are and their weaknesses. While we have a tendency to think 'I won't do that' - be humbled, because you will probably do something else instead. Ask your parents and parents in-law, what they wish they could have done differently and what they are pleased about in raising you and your hubby.

One key word, to me, is 'communicate'. I do not only mean with each other but also with this new baby when he or she comes.

There is always the possibility that you will not be given this wonderful gift. We have no 'rights' to be parents and God, in His greater purpose, may not have planned children for you. This is very hard to take and to hear. Examine your hearts before God. Lay your whole lives before Him. Ask Him how He wishes to use you both in His service and be willing to trust Him and obey Him in whatever way He leads you both. Perhaps God will open up other opportunities to you that would never have happened if you had a family. I know this is a whole other topic and, if you want, we can explore this together some other time.

In the meantime, I will pray for you that God would bless you with a family. I pray that you are both entrusted with new life: the most precious of gifts. I look forward to hearing from you soon.

With love,

XXX

PS – Personally I do not particularly like 'Aunt or Auntie'. I will train any child of yours to call me by my first name. I just thought I would add that part. Love and hugs x

1 Samuel 1.26-27 And she said, Oh my lord, *as* thy soul liveth, my lord, I *am* the woman that stood by thee here, praying

unto the Lord. For this child I prayed; and the Lord hath given me my petition which I asked of him:

Genesis 18.10;Psalm 20.4;Psalm 37.4; Psalm 62.8; Psalm 119.59; Psalm 127.3-5a; Proverbs 3.5-6; Isaiah 54.1; Isaiah 58.11;Lamentations 3.40; St. Luke 11.9-10; 2 Corinthians 13.5; Galatians 2.20; James 1.22.

First Baby

My dear friend,

I am just so pleased, thrilled, delighted to hear of the news of your first child. May God bless this little one. May His face shine on him and may he grow in the grace of the Lord Jesus and in his knowledge of Him.

Any child is a miracle. When you know about all the things that can go wrong at birth, you will know this to be true. Yet, your child is a gift: a gift from God. You do not own your child. You have been entrusted with this precious one. As the potter moulds the clay into its shape, so you are entrusted to shape your child as he grows. Teach him right from wrong, teach him to read the Bible and say his prayers. Teach him how to say 'sorry' and 'I forgive you' and mean it. Teach him how to be kind, generous, loving and full of service and love.

When you leave him with someone else for the first time, do not fret or worry. Our Heavenly Father has His angels looking after him. He is only yours until he is old enough to start making his own way in this world. So teach him how to be independent. He is a gift – do not waste that gift.

I am sure that you are over the moon yet also exhausted. Who could believe how such a tiny, miraculous human being can be so all-consuming of your time and energies? Don't try to plan too far ahead. Ensure that you stop and wonder at his beauty. Gaze in his eyes, when they are open. Laugh at his smiles. Enjoy the very essence of his being. Everyone says that babies grow so quickly and that is true. Do not wish his life away but enjoy every moment. Capture these special times in your heart. Store them up there to remember in the years to come. Sleep when he sleeps so you are rested to enjoy him again. This time will pass. Enjoy it while you have it.

One of these days, I will see you and meet your new son. I long to see him: to see if he has your eyes, or his Dad's nose and all the other family similarities. He is beautifully and wonderfully made.

Until that time, I send you all my love and prayers.

Your friend,

X

Luke 2.19 But Mary kept all these things, and pondered *them* in her heart.

Genesis 1.27; Exodus 23.20; Numbers 6.24-26; 1 Samuel 2.26; Psalm 127.3-5a; Psalm 145.5; Isaiah 64.8; Jeremiah 1.5; St. Matthew 6.25; St. Luke 2.52;Ephesians 5.1;1 Peter 5.7.

Moving House

O my, how very exciting! I cannot wait to see your new house. When is your entry date? Did you get the one that you were telling me about? I have thousands of questions for you, of course, but overall, I am just so very, very pleased for you.

People say a house is just bricks and mortar. A building is that. Some buildings are awe inspiring and others quite mundane but it takes some very special people to make a home out of bricks and mortar.

So what is a home? I think we could spend many hours discussing that. We all assume that home is a safe space but we also know that this is not always the case. We can assume that home is where we thrive and grow and yet, so often, it is where we first experience the cutting words of others, who love us, and the constant put-downs of our family. So, idealising home is not very realistic, is it?

However, our earthly, Christian homes, should surely be something different, something better? A place where we encourage the ones that we love; where we build each other up; where we learn how to love and serve our Lord together; where we rebuke each other, stop each other from pride and sin and learn what are our talents and giftings.

I really must share these verses with you. I always give them to people who are getting married or, like you, are moving house. I love them!

Proverbs 24 verses 3 and 4 says: 'Through wisdom a house is built, and by understanding it is established; by knowledge the rooms are filled with all precious and pleasant riches.'

God told King Solomon to ask Him for anything and He would give it. You will remember the story. Solomon asked God for wisdom. If you do a search for the words wisdom, knowledge and understanding within the Bible, you will see that these three words are often used together.

So I pray that your new home will be filled with wisdom: wisdom to make good decisions; wisdom to choose your battles (ha! ha! – you know what I mean!) and when to let things take their course; wisdom to know when to do things, when to rest; when to be alone and when to invite others into your home. Wisdom relates to choices and I pray that you will make good choices about your money, time and communications with others.

Understanding is an interesting subject. To understand means that you have to put yourself into the shoes of the other person and see things from their perspective. You will have new neighbours who may not share your values. Will you understand when they say or do things that you do not agree with? Will you be wise to know when to speak up and when to be silent?

Jesus told us that where our treasure is, there our hearts will be also. The verses in Proverbs talk about the contents of your home being filled with all precious and pleasant riches. Are you being told to spend lots of money (that you certainly will not have just now!) on expensive interior decorating? I do not really think that is what these verses are saying. I think these verses are saying that your rooms will be filled with precious and pleasant riches – by knowledge. So how do these concepts relate to each other?

Knowledge means you will fill your rooms with what edifies, builds up and encourages and not what destroys. Knowledge means that you will build up lots of happy and valuable memories through the times spent with others in your rooms. Knowledge means that, ever mindful of your budget (yes!) and your responsibilities, you will fill your rooms with things that are pleasing to you but not so expensive that you are not able to live in your rooms.

Overall, this wisdom, understanding and knowledge all come from the Lord Himself. He will fill your home. May the fragrance of the Lord Jesus Christ pervade your home that it is a haven of rest to the weary, a place of solace and comfort to the hurting, where the lazy are challenged and the upset are comforted.

Now, what are your timescales? Do you want a hand with packing things? Taking things to the recycling centre? May I provide a meal for you the day you actually move? Do you want me to sit in your old house for the meters to be read before you leave?

I am just so very pleased for you. New ventures!

Tons of love,

X

2 Corinthians 2.14-15 Now thanks *be* unto God, which always causeth us to triumph in Christ, and maketh manifest the savour of his knowledge by us in every place. For we are unto God a sweet savour of Christ, in them that are saved, and in them that perish.

1 Kings 3.9; Proverbs 2.6; Proverbs 4.6-7; Proverbs 24.3-4; Isaiah 11.2; St. Matthew 6.19-21;St. John 16.33; Romans 15.2; Philippians 4.8; Hebrews 10.24-25; James 3.17.

Children's Choices

O dear, O dear. It is so hard to let go, isn't it? It is so hard to watch our children make choices that we know will end up in heartbreak, sorrow, pain, tears. How can we help them when they will not listen to us nor will they do what we advise?

I think first and foremost we constantly bring them before the Lord in prayer. We need to persist in prayer and never give up. The Lord loves to hear our prayers and to answer them: our responsibility is to pray. We also need to humble ourselves before God and be prepared to listen to what He has to say to us. Recently I have felt that the Lord has been repeatedly telling me to wait – His timing not mine, His way – not mine and that I have to just be there walking alongside my friend and leave Him to work His purposes out.

Secondly, we have to model wise choices and tell our children how we made those choices so that they do not just see what we have done but also our thinking behind our decision making. Tell them where you felt you made the wrong decision and how God used that. Tell them about His signs and wonders and directions by which you knew that God was leading you in a certain way.

Years ago I learned the art of questioning. Our Lord uses questioning a lot in His communications with others. By asking open-ended questions of your child, you are not being confrontational but rather trying to engage them in dialogue that will help them make their own decisions. Part of that would be encouraging them to think through the implications of their actions. 'You might like to think about…' is one of my stock phrases. My children can now see it coming (ha ha!) and I can see them inwardly groaning.

Like the father of the prodigal son, when our children make wrong choices, it is crucial that we are not just waiting, but running to meet them, with outstretched arms for when they return. We must not be judgemental. Only the Lord will judge us. We need to mirror unconditional love as He has to us. Children need to experiment and know that the safety net is there to catch them.

I used to pray that my children would see the evils of this world but not be tarnished by it. In other words, see what happens when people live a Godless life but not actively engage in it. Regardless, we all fail. We are all sinners and there is a way back to God when we mess up.

Lastly, we need to entrust our children into the Lord's safe keeping. The first time they walk home from school by themselves? The Lord's goodness and mercy are following them. The Lord created them, we entrust them to His safe keeping. He will give His angels charge concerning them. Hand them over to the Lord and watch and see what He will do.

It is in our nature to want to do more for our children, to protect them from others etc. and yet it is only in the engagement with others that they grow and learn for themselves that the Lord is good - He saves them that trust in Him.

Children, a humbling experience, a testing experience, a privilege, a pleasure and they are an absolute joy! They are not ours – only given to us on loan. Let them go into God's loving arms. There is no better place for them to be. And stand and watch what the Lord will do!

Love, your friend

x

Psalm 91.11 For he shall give his angels charge over thee, to keep thee in all thy ways.

Deuteronomy 6.7; 1 Kings 19.13b; Psalm 23.6; Psalm 27.14; Psalm 127.3; Proverbs 22.6; Isaiah 33.22; Jeremiah 33.3; Nahum 1.7; St. Matthew 6.13; St. Matthew 7.1-2; St. Matthew 16.13; St. Luke 15.20; St. Luke 18.1-8a; St. John 3.16; St. John 8.10; St. John 15.9; Philippians 4.6; James 4.10; 1 John 1.9.

Achievements

Weehee! Get the balloons out! Get the party organised! We are going to celebrate! I am just so very, very pleased for you. Well done my dear pal!

You have worked so hard for this achievement. You have pushed yourself (and others ha ha!) to complete all that you have done. You have given up so much – especially your social life. When can I book you in for a coffee, cake and chat session? You have been focused and driven and now you have got it.

Many, many congratulations!

I never doubted that you could do it. I thank God for this! I was just concerned that the price would have been too much.

So, let the celebrations begin and after that, what next?

By the grace of God you have added another string to your bow. With a new enabling comes new responsibilities. You have been given much and so much more will be required. So, how do you think our Lord wants you to use this new experience further for His glory?

Wait for the Lord. Don't rush into new ventures too quickly. Unless you have a clear sense of His guidance, wait, and He will lead you. Remember this new thing is not for you only but also for the service of others. Whatever you do, do it heartily as unto the Lord, and not to man. So, serve the Lord with gladness, come before Him with singing. We are all joining you in this celebration!

I hope to see you really soon. I am so proud of you and so pleased for you.

Love from Your friend,

X

Luke 12.48b For unto whomsoever much is given, of him shall be much required: and to whom men have committed much, of him they will ask the more.

Psalm 25.5; Psalm 29.2; Psalm 37.7; Psalm 100.2; Psalm 130.5; Psalm 150.6; Romans 9.23, 24; Romans 14.8; 1 Corinthians 12.14; 1 Corinthians 12.27; Ephesians 5.20.

Coping with Teenagers

Love them or loathe them, we were all a teenager at one time or another. A dear friend once said to me 'I will not make the same mistakes as my mum....I will just make different ones!' and I think when we consider our teenagers, without realising it, we have our own stories as a reference point.

What did you get up to as a teenager that you regret? You will probably try and stop your own from doing the same.

What did you get up as a teenager that you loved? You will probably try and encourage your teenager to do the same.

Can you see what I mean? Yet, your teenager is unique. There has not been anyone, before or after, who is the same. Your teenager has her own personality. Yes you can see yourself in her and your husband but she is not you, nor him, she is herself. So you can only guide and direct and suggest and encourage her to make good choices.

Try and look at the world from her perspective. She is not us. She is subject to a whole range of pressures that we never had. Social media has a lot of good and bad about it. Her life is lived in a gold fish bowl and none of us can stand up to that scrutiny. Be her guard and her guide. There are lots of resources to guide you about the use and abuse of social media. Become familiar with them as you never know when you will need them.

Teenagers stretch your own emotions in ways you never thought possible. You thought you were a reasonable, well adjusted person and yet, one conversation with your teenager can evoke the most unbelievable emotions. I think their job is to press our buttons – all the wrong ones. It is such a challenging time. Like navigating through treacle at times but it can also bring great rewards.

Friendships are so very, very important in teenage years and yet these are the things that you cannot influence as much as when she was in primary school. You might not know her friends' parents and their interests etc. However, you can try to get to know her friends. Invite her friends for tea. Offer lifts to and from parties. Keep your home open to others so her friends know that they have a safe place to go to if they need it. Don't try to befriend her friends. You are her mum. Her friends will see you as their friend's mum. Be that unique person in their lives. Step back but be there if you are needed.

Above it all, keep the communications open. You are the adult even when you feel like screaming and throwing things; even when you feel like casting her off and disowning her. Even when you feel like throwing her out the house……YOU are the adult. You are the adult who models Father God to her. You are the only one, as well as your hubby, who demonstrates unconditional love. Hard love, at times, but you need to keep communications open and of course, pray continually.

Consider life from their perspective. They have hormones raging and one day are as crabbit and irritable as a prickly hedgehog and the next they are all over you with hugs and words of love and affirmation. Speak with her and help her to understand how her hormones impact on her feelings and behaviours. Help her learn about her body and how it is changing and what this means.

Oh and by the way, 'I hate you, Mum', is all part of a teenager's vocabulary. Hate is the opposite side of the love coin. It means she feels really, really deeply for you. Please do not react with threats. Once said, something cannot be taken back. A soft answer turns away wrath. I would suggest something like, 'I am sorry that is how you feel about me. It does not change how I feel about you and I love you with all my heart'. This is just one way to keep communications open.

Like her early years, these years too will pass and throughout it all, together we will thank our good Lord who has looked after us all and our teenagers.

What fun times!

With love,

Your friend

X

Ephesians 4.29 Let no corrupt communication proceed out of your mouth, but that which is good to the use of edifying, that it may minister grace unto the hearers.

Psalm 23.6; Psalm 139.13-16; Proverbs 15.1; Proverbs 18.24; Proverbs 22.6; Jeremiah 31.33; St. Luke 15.17-20; Galatians 1.15-16; Ephesians 6.4; Colossians 3.12, 21; 1 Thessalonians

5.16-18; 2 Timothy 2.23-24; Titus 3.9; Hebrews 13.2; 3 John 11.

Going on Holiday

So your bags are packed and you are all ready to go. Did I hear you laugh? Yes, it always sounds good in practice and then you realise the thousand and one things that must be done before you leave for your holiday. Not only are you packing for yourself, you are packing for the rest of the family as well. Is that not so? Roll on the years when they can pack their own things. So as well as planning for the week away (is it really only one week?) you are also thinking of the things that must be done before you go.

Part of that pressure is that you do not want to return home to dirty washing that was there before you left. Part of that pressure is that, should something happen to you when you are away, someone else may need to access the house for things and you cannot possibly go away with a dirty house! We all do it. Is it our pride that makes us work like that – or what?

Someone once said to me that the holiday starts from the minute you leave the house. The journey is part of the holiday. So I pray that your journey is smooth, there is no travel sickness (Oh no), no hiccups on the way and that you all arrive in one piece and begin to relax.

Yet, I know that the first few days of the holiday will be fractious. It is almost as if someone has said, 'You are on holiday – relax', as if it were an order. We cannot relax to order. I know, as I have tried it and it does not work. So please, please be kind on yourself, to yourself and to the rest of the family. It takes a few days to unwind to a different pace of life.

A holiday is really a holy day. So what is a holy day? It is all modelled on the creation story and how God made the world in six days and He rested on the seventh day. God did not need to rest, because He is God, but He did. He set in place rhythms of living that are good for creation and good for our bodies. As God rested, so we need to rest. Every seventh day we need to rest. Add into this that we take holidays, rest from work, and we are so very fortunate to have this gift of 'holy days'. Days to rest; not to quickly look at work emails nor to respond to social media, but to rest.

Coupled with this, when God rested, it was because everything that he had made He saw was good. All creation, all the land, plants, animals, birds, human beings (not human doings) were all good. There is something in our resting where we need to see the good: in each other; in our surroundings; in the beauty of this earth and this planet. The sun and moon that you see in a different country is the same sun and moon that we see back home. The earth and the universe are good. Be so very grateful for the good that we experience and can see and give God thanks for it all.

I challenge you to see the 'good' in each day – be it a sunset, a relaxing time with the family, that lovely ice cream that you had by the seashore or just the fact that you all got on together.

Holidays, time for rest, relaxation, recuperation and counting our blessings and thanking God for all the good things that He has done and is doing. It is a time for a different pace, different experiences and different time frames. Enjoy it! Work and all its pressures will be here when you return but as you take time out, relax, enjoy your holy day and be thankful. God bless you, dear. Please do not send me a postcard (as you are on holiday). I look forward to catching up with you when you return.

Love, prayers and blessings dear friend,

X

1 Timothy 4.4-5 For every creature of God *is* good, and nothing to be refused, if it be received with thanksgiving: For it is sanctified by the word of God and prayer.

Genesis 1.31; Genesis 2.2-3; Exodus 33.14; Psalm 55.6; Psalm 107.21; Isaiah 14.7; Isaiah 26.3-4; Isaiah 30.15; Isaiah 63.14; St. Matthew 11. 28-30; St. Mark 6.31; 1 Thessalonians 5.18; Hebrews 4.9-11; James 4.6; 1 Peter 5.6.

Letting go of Your Children

So, it is happening after all then? She is leaving home. I know you will be delighted for her but also terrified for her. It is an exciting time for you both and the rest of the family.

'Children are God's heritage, the womb's fruit His reward'. I am sorry to burst your bubble but you know that she was never yours in the first place. The Lord formed her in your womb. The Lord knitted her together in the secret place. The Lord made her unique, and not you. He made her in His image although she does bear an uncanny likeness to you in lots of ways. You are only her custodian and guardian in this life; a precious gift from God.

I do have to say, though, that you have been an excellent mum to her. You have been a brilliant role model. You have loved her unconditionally. You have given her tough love when it was needed and you have both had such fun over the years that it has been brilliant to watch. Do you remember the time that you both got stuck coming down that slide in the park? I thought there was going to be an accident as we laughed so much. No honestly, you have guided her and steered her. You have shown her how to stand up for herself and how to be gracious and humble.

You have prayed faithfully for her all the days of her life – and even before she was born. She sees Christ in you. She knows that you intercede for her, with the Lord. She is gradually taking her own steps in faith which is great to watch. She is surrounded by so many people supporting her and cheering her on her way that she cannot help but do well.

So, my dear friend, let her go. Please do not try and stop her. It is all part of growing up. She has now got to learn how to fall down on her own and how to dust herself down and stand up afterwards. You cannot always be there for her. She can only move onto the next stage of maturity in this life by taking more responsibility for her actions and making her own decisions with the accountability involved in all of them.

You are not losing her. You will gain her as an independent adult and that brings even more closeness with it. Let her go to find herself; to be herself; to establish herself. You have done so well up until now. Please do not try and squash her at this stage.

Get a box and start to fill it with some things that she will need in her new abode. Put in some tea and coffee, biscuits, sugar, some mugs, teaspoons, plates, cutlery. Now add some tea towels, some washing up liquid, some cleaning products and dusters and cloths. Add some matches, candles, a small sewing pack, a small first aid kit. All things that she will need but I can assure you she will never get round to purchasing for herself. You did show her how to sew on a button, didn't you?

Give her some space. It will be hard. Let her be the first to contact you. Try not to bombard her with messages and questions. When she wants you to know how she is getting on, she will tell you. Don't expect her to visit you regularly. Remember that her new abode is hers now, not yours and not her childhood 'home'. You will be a guest in her home so act as one. There is great liberty in that. She will need to make the cups of tea for you, for a change, and you are not responsible for clearing and cleaning it. Honest! It is her space, so step back.

Oh, and by the way, don't give up her room at home yet. She might want to return and, at the moment, her room needs to be ready for her.

Great times, m'dear! Great times! You actually might find yourself enjoying a wee bit more freedom and liberty to do as you want for a change. The shopping bill will be less. The laundry much less and the house will stay cleaner for longer. So more time for you – and me – to do lunch and have coffees.

God bless. You are a fantastic mother! You will always be her mother. She does not need to live with you for that to be the case. Free her for this next stage and in that process, you will also free yourself.

Much love,

X

Proverbs 31.15, 20, 25-29 She riseth also while it is yet night, and giveth meat to her household, and a portion to her maidens. She stretcheth out her hand to the poor; yea, she reacheth forth her hands to the needy. Strength and honour *are* her clothing; and she shall rejoice in time to come. She openeth her mouth with wisdom; and in her tongue *is* the law of kindness. She looketh well to the ways of her household, and eateth not the bread of idleness. Her children arise up, and call her blessed; her husband *also*, and he praiseth her. Many daughters have done virtuously, but thou excellest them all.

1 Samuel 1.26-27; Psalm 127.3; Psalm 139.13-16; Song of Songs 8.2a; Jeremiah 1.5; 2 Timothy 1.5; Titus 2.3-5; Hebrews 12.1,2; 2 Peter 3.18.

Midlife

Hiya, how are you doing? It was so good to see you recently. I love your new hairstyle. The cut and the colour really suit you. I was reflecting on what we were saying about this stage in life and just wanted to share some of my thoughts with you. No doubt we will continue this conversation when next we meet.

My first thought was, at what stage in life are we 'grown up?' Having both of our parents still living, for which we thank God, means that we are still daughters, as well as mothers. So, in some ways we are still our 'mothers' little girls'. I know I certainly revert to type when I am with my mum. She would be horrified at some of the things I do, say and the responsibilities that I carry at work, in the Church and at home. It is easier not to tell her. Ha Ha!

In some ways it is good not to be too serious about life but in others, our responsibilities can feel overwhelming. I suppose in work, we are grown-ups by what we are doing. At home, we are the responsible adults to our children (If they only knew our insecurities etc.). I suppose the difference comes with our parents who still see us as their children so maybe we just have to accept that, to them, we are not grown up and just have to navigate our way round our relationships with them. I know this will change as they get older, frail and needing more support so maybe we should just accept things as they are just now and enjoy this stage.

However, this stage in life is not easy. I wonder if life ever gets easier. So how do we cope with the business of life at our stage? I think we both want to give our children all the opportunities that we had, and more, but it can be hard to work, run a home, take the young ones to Guides, Brownies, swimming, music lessons and the like and still find some time to prepare for Sunday School and do housework. Something has to give and, for me, it is my social life. As you and I are so alike, I am therefore assuming that this applies to you as well. So, how do we cope?

I do think that there is a definite place for using our time, energies, skills and abilities well. I do wonder if we are meant to be so busy? I do not see that urgency of activity in Jesus' life. Nor do I see that this is how our Lord works all down history. I know that we should walk in step with his Spirit and learn the unforced rhythms of His grace so I ask myself, and you through this letter, are we on the hamster wheel of this world or are we walking as the Lord would have us walk? How about a wee bit of accountability here? Shall we both agree to stop something or do something more positive in our lives to ensure that we are walking as God wants us to walk and not as other people would make us walk? This is just a wee suggestion to be chewed over when we meet for our walk next week.

How do we adjust to the physical changes in our bodies that happen mid life?

Because I like to think my mind is still young, I make the assumption that my body is also still young. So, I do get seriously disappointed in my body. What a joke! Yes, I am battling the weight gain that happens to us all as we get older (there is that word again). I suppose energy in and expenditure out do not quite equate as I jump into the car to take the kids to the next activity. I see parts of my body now letting me down (you know which bits they are!) which seems to emphasise that we are 'at that age' which everyone seems to be going on about. Gosh, if we are not worrying about jobs, partners, mortgages and the likes, we are then worrying about our physical frames. We do need to remember that the Lord has made us. He knows our frame. He remembers that we are but dust. Still, the Lord is not finished with us yet and, like Paul, we may be given things to bear so that God can show His strength and grace through our weakness. However, we do have a responsibility to care for these bodies. After all, they are His temple.

Where is Jesus in all this?

I suppose, that through it all, we should cast our worries and cares on Jesus. I suppose we need to learn to let Him lead us and not be swayed by the expectations of other people. He did promise us His Holy Spirit to be our guide and counsellor and we can not only receive wisdom and grace by His Spirit but also the strength to carry on. We shall rise on wings of eagles. However, like you, I want to be sure that I am still walking in the narrow way that leads to life and not the broad way that leads to destruction.

Sorry this letter is so long; apologies for my ramblings. I find it helpful to write things down onto paper that I can then re-read and think through more. I do thank God that He is so patient with me in all things. He knows that I am a work in progress. I just hope and pray that I am malleable to His potter's hand, moulding and shaping me at this stage in my life into the person that He wants me to be: who shows His love to others and reflects His glory.

You have tempted me to change my hair style. Regardless, I know that there are changes I need to make in my lifestyle, thoughts and attitudes and I am aiming to take every thought captive to be more obedient to our Saviour.

I am really looking forward to seeing you again.

With much love,

XX

Psalm 71.5-6 For thou *art* my hope, O Lord God: *thou art* my trust from my youth. By thee have I been holden up from the womb: thou art he that took me out of my mother's bowels: my praise *shall be* continually of thee.

Psalm 68.19; Psalm 71.18; Isaiah 40.31; Isaiah 46.4; St. Matthew 6.30; St. Matthew 7.13-14; St. Matthew 10.37-39; St. Matthew 11. 28-30; St. Mark 6.31; 1 Corinthians 6.19-20; 1 Corinthians 10.31; 2 Corinthians 3.18; 2 Corinthians 10.5; 2 Corinthians 12.9; Galatians 6.9; Ephesians 3.20-21; Ephesians 6.1-4; Philippians 3.13-14.

Acute Ill Health

My dear friend,

I am very sorry to hear that you are so poorly at the moment. It is awful when your life grinds to a very quick halt and, knowing you, you will be thinking of all the things that need to be done over the next few days and weeks. It looks like you need to hand these over to others at the moment. I do pray that you are receiving the correct help – medically, physically, emotionally and spiritually.

Someone once said to me 'God orders our stops as well as our goes' and He has stopped you now, for whatever reason. There is nothing you can do, except stop, rest, sleep and recover. You cannot rush this. You need to give in. Your body and mind need to stop to allow your body to heal itself as much as it can. In times like this, you can feel as if you want to die. Do you know that it is perfectly normal to feel like that? Others have wished it, but, when they have recovered, they are ready for life again. Give in to the tiredness and doze and sleep. If you do get up, sit and read, watch your favourite film, listen to some music but please do not push yourself to do anything. It will only delay your recovery.

This illness is for a season and it will pass. Ask the Lord what He wants to lay on your heart at the moment. Does He want you to rest in His love; draw closer to Him, to feel His loving arms around you, to know your head is being held by His loving hands? Does He want you to look around and consider your neighbours and how you can best pray for them? Does He want you to receive care and blessing from others – when you are so quick to give of yourself but maybe need to learn to receive? Does He want to shower His blessing on you but you have been too busy to notice up until now?

Regardless, the Lord bless and keep you. I will pop round with some chicken soup tomorrow. Everyone says it is very good for healing.

In the meantime, rest up. You will soon be up and about again and we can catch up when you are able.

Love you loads,

Your friend,

XX

2 Kings 20.2, 5 Then he turned his face to the wall, and prayed unto the Lord, saying, …'Turn again, and tell Hezekiah the captain of my people, Thus saith the Lord, the God of David thy father, I have seen they tears: behold I will heal thee: on the third day thou shalt go up unto the house of the Lord.

Numbers 22.21-23; 31; Deuteronomy 33.27a; 1 Kings 19.4-8; Psalm 103.3; Psalm 134.3; Ecclesiastes 3.1; St. John 14.1; Galatians 5.25; 1 Thessalonians 5.11.

Chronic Ill Health

Dear friend,

Who am I to tell you how to live your life? I have not walked in your shoes and do not fully understand all that you are going through. I know that when you are well, you do well and enjoy life. I also know that the dark shadow of ill-health hovers on your shoulder and at any day, any time you are pulled low with ill health. So I rejoice with you when you are well and able and I pray with you when you are feeling frail and ill.

What does our Lord say in all this? I could quote 'My grace is sufficient for thee : for my strength is made perfect in weakness' but I know you have heard all that before. I could quote Jeremiah 29.11 but again, you know that verse so well, how can I quote it for you? I could say nothing, like Job's friends did – for a week - and then they started to blame him for his own ill health.

So, I will say nothing. I pray for you. I pray that our Lord would heal you. We both know that He can heal you and we both know that this long term illness is not normally healed by God in this way.

I pray that our Lord would be so very present with you that you do not want to leave His company. I pray that when you are wracked with pain, that the presence of His Holy Spirit is a salve to your bones. I pray that when you feel down and fed up by it all, that you will know the joy of the Lord as your strength and His heavenly peace. I pray that through it all, you will know His peace that passes all understanding; His presence that goes before you and gives you rest; His day by day encouragement and support.

I pray that as you live with the hour by hour, day by day uncertainty, that you are a living example to us all on how to learn to trust Him with all things.

I pray that you know you are loved with an everlasting love. Your name is written in His book of life and that you are held within the palm of His hands.

The Lord bless you and keep you. May His face shine upon you and be gracious unto you. The Lord lift up His countenance upon you and give you His peace.

With love and prayers,

Your friend,

X

Psalm 23.4 Yea, though I walk through the valley of the shadow of death, I will fear no evil: for thou *art* with me; thy rod and thy staff they comfort me.

Numbers 6.24-26; Nehemiah 8.10b; Job 2.11-13; Psalm 20.7; Psalm 40.1; Psalm 42.11; Isaiah 49.16; Jeremiah 29.11-14a; St. Matthew 6.6; St. Matthew 18.20; St. Luke 10.20; St. John 14.26; Romans 12.15; Romans 15.13; 2 Corinthians 12.7-9; Philippians 1.3; 1 Thessalonians 1. 2.

Missing You

I know that we are best of friends. I know that we have shared so many intimacies over the years. I know that you care deeply for me and my family and you know that I feel the same about yours. I also know that sometimes, we really do not speak about how much we mean to each other because actually, it is very hard to put into words.

I know that you are going through a really hard time at the moment. You are being pulled in so many directions. I also know that you are very good with boundaries and so the constant pressure and stress that you are under will be challenging these same boundaries and this, as well, will be causing you even more pressure and stress.

In no way do I want to add to these pressures and stresses. So, first be assured of my love and prayers for you at this time. I am not sure how I can help you, but I can pray for you. I hope that you will know the strength and enabling that only comes from our Lord as you navigate the treacle in which you are mired. He is our strength and our stay.

However, I do want to say, that I miss you! I miss your company. I miss your voice. I miss hearing your angst, your laughter and your wonderful whacky view on life that always leaves me laughing! I really do value you as a person, as a friend, as a sister in Christ and as a bosom buddy. I am here for you whenever there is a space that you want to fill with me. In the meantime, please be assured of my ongoing love and affection.

This too will pass and you will again thrive, instead of just surviving. I am waiting for that phone call, text, email, whatever to say, ' How do you fancy meeting up?'. God bless and keep you in His loving arms and support and enable you. Until that time, miss you pal.

XXX

Mizpah

Genesis 31.49 And Mizpah; for he said, The Lord watch between me and thee, when we are absent one from another.

Deuteronomy 33.27a; Joshua 1.9; 1 Samuel 18.3; Nehemiah 8.10b; Psalm 34.18-19; Psalm 68.19; Proverbs 18.10; Isaiah 40.29; Isaiah 41.10; 1 Corinthians 15.58; 2 Corinthians 9.8; Ephesians 1.3, 15-17; Philippians 1.7-8; Colossians 1.3; Colossians 3.15;Philemon 4.

Growing Old

Oh baha humbug... I do not like this growing old business. I know I ought to embrace it, be thankful that I have lived this long, but I am tired of this body and how it is failing me.

It takes me longer to recover now after a good walk. I find myself falling asleep in my chair in the middle of the afternoon. When the grandchildren visit, I am exhausted when they leave. Parts of my body are now doubly gravitated (I know that is not a word) in that there are rifts and valleys in parts of my body that used to be smooth and taut. I sometimes struggle to find the correct words. I need glasses to read and hearing aids to hear but I am thankful that I have my own teeth to eat. My knees and ankles groan if I have been sitting for too long and my hair is losing its colour, texture and bounce. So Baha humbug.

Ok, dear friend, so how are we meant to approach this time of life, as Christian women?

I am getting older. I thank God that I am still here and able to participate in life and in the Church. I do not have as much energy as I used to but I have more time to pray for others and I do enjoy a good long chatter with my Lord and Saviour. I think I am a wee bit wiser now and know not to bother wasting my limited energies on things that are not worth it. Does it matter if there are some spelling mistakes in the monthly newsletter? Has the world come to an end? Yes, it is nice if it can be read without seeing the obvious mistakes but in the bigger scheme of things, the person writing it should be encouraged and not reprimanded.

Yes, I get tired more easily but isn't it lovely when some of the younger people ask our advice on various issues? They recognise the lived experience that we have from which they can learn. You and I do not need to go through it all again – we have been there and done it, but we can support and encourage those who are currently going through other aspects of life. I suppose not all older people have wisdom or learned from their experiences but I like to think that we have, as so many others want to learn from us.

We have both been so blessed in our walk with the Lord to see our prayers answered. Sometimes these have not been answered as we would like but, on reflection, the answer has been the right one. Is it not wonderful that we can pass such experiences onto others and encourage them when their prayers are not answered or not answered as they would like?

One good thing about growing older, I am no longer expected to move any more chairs at the Church. This is a real bonus. I know that in heaven Jesus sits at the right hand of the Father so there must be chairs there, but on earth, the time of heaving and humping church chairs from one place to another is ended. O hallelujah for that!

So, growing old, dear friend? We can do this together. Our Lord is gracious and compassionate. He has used older people all down the ages; Abraham; Moses; Anna. He has yet a purpose and use for us. So let's embrace this stage in life, with all its challenges and frailties and look and see what the Lord will do through us, with us and for us. Take heart and pass the cream scones please!

Love and nonsense X

1 Kings 12.6 And king Rehoboam consulted with the old men, that stood before Solomon his father while he yet lived, and said, How do ye advise that I may answer this people?

Genesis 25.8; Deuteronomy 34.7; Job 5.26; Job 12.12; Psalm 66.19; Psalm 71.18; Psalm 92.14; Psalm 145.8; Proverbs 23.22; Isaiah 46.4; St. Mark 11.24; St. Mark 16.19; St. Luke 2.36; St. John 21.18; Acts 6.4; 2 Corinthians 4.16; James 5.16.

Caring for Older Family Members

So the roles have reversed. When did this happen? How did this happen? Just gradually, over the months and years, old age and frailty have sneaked in the door and your dearly beloved mum has become more vulnerable and less able to live independently. Old age is not for the faint hearted. In the meantime, your own role has changed.

I have watched you. It started with you taking over the Christmas present shopping. 'Well,' you said, 'It is easier. I know what they all want and I am doing my own shopping on line so I might as well get Mum's shopping while I am here. It's easier all round.'

Gradually you took on more cleaning in her home. I am so glad that you saw sense there and got someone in to do this. It is bad enough trying to keep our own homes clean and tidy when we are both working without taking on your mum's as well.

Then she had that doctor's appointment and could not recall what the doctor had said. I could see your frustration building up as the doctor would not talk to you, due to 'patient confidentiality'. This meant you had to arrange another appointment with your Mum, taking time off work and going with her to hear what the doctor had said.

I am so glad that you arranged for the Power of Attorney and that it was invoked as soon as it was arranged. It is hard. It is very hard. However, you now have the legal authority to make decisions for your mum: to pay her bills, to set up appointments to plan her future. And suddenly, it has happened. You are now her carer.

What is the first, chief role of a carer? I should give you time to write your answers on a postcard, however, me being me, I will give you my views. The first role of a carer is to look after herself. Not what you expected? If you do not look after yourself, then you are no use to anyone. So, do not jump every time your mum phones. Find out what the problem is, then decide how it is to be sorted and who will sort it. It is not all down to you. When you are offered respite care, take it. It will help to keep you going for longer and Mum might actually like a change of scenery.

Ask you brother and sister to step up. Could one of them look after Mum for an evening on a regular basis to give you time for yourself? Have you spoken with social services to see what other support there is for Mum at this stage?

Hard, I know, but Mum is not going to improve anymore; she is only going to deteriorate therefore pace yourself – and her. This is the time when, if there was anything that she has always wanted to do, do it now. Don't wait for another six months. She might not be so able in six months' time. Seize the moment and act now.

Your true friends are all here to support you: to take you out of yourself; to sit quietly with you; to help with Mum, if she will allow us. Your true friends do not go away just because your situation has changed. This too is for a season. A special, unique season, so enjoy our time with Mum.

Yes, the roles have changed. You are still her daughter as well as her carer. You are always her daughter and her child. Love your mum. Love yourself. Love our Lord.

Happy to take you out for a walk, a coffee, a cry, a moan, a chat! We just need to arrange a time and date.

Love you, X

Ecclesiastes 3.1 To every *thing there is* a season, and a time to every purpose under the heaven:

Genesis 46.5-6; St. Matthew 7.12; St. Matthew 22.37-39; St. Matthew 25.40; St. John 13.14-15; St. John 19.26-27; St. John 21.18; Ephesians 6.1-3; Hebrews 13.5b-6; 1 Peter 1.12.

Death of a parent

My dear friend

I was so sorry to hear that your father had died. He had a long, fulfilling life and I will always remember his stories about his time in the army. He loved those days: the friendships that still last from the bonds created through some adverse times. He appreciated the discipline that the army gave him and, of course, it was while he was home on leave that he met and eventually married your mum.

Along with his stories, I will also remember his silent presence in your home. He was just there. Not intrusively there but just present. I knew that he loved it when we would all crowd into your sitting room for some TV programme or to swap stories and he would take his cup of tea and wander through to the kitchen to give us space. He never complained but rather gave out a serene welcome to all us young folk and clearly we were not a bother to him. A real saint!

Over the years, I watched how his values and ethics influenced your own perspective of life which was a credit to him. He was an upright gentleman, full of grace and truth and exuded manners in a way I wish that some of our men could learn from him today. Nothing was any bother to him. He was kindness itself.

Rest assured that he was always very proud of you and spoke of you with such affection. He knew where you were, what you were doing and always referred to your many achievements with such pride in his voice that it was clear he loved and adored you. You were the apple of his eye.

You did well in caring for him as much as you did in these latter years. I know that you gave up a lot of your own life to be there for your father. He did not ask it, he did not expect it but out of love for him, you gave and gave of yourself. You could not have done more. May you find some comfort in knowing that you honoured your father throughout your whole life and this came from a deep love for him.

You will miss him dearly. Take comfort that he is now asleep in the Lord and that you will see him again someday. We are told that, 'He that believeth in me, though he were dead, yet shall he live and whosoever liveth and believeth in me shall never die'. He has gone before and you will see him again.

May the God of all comforts comfort you in your grief and may His Holy Spirit surround you and uphold you in these hard days.

Please send my deepest condolences to your mum and brother. I will write to them separately.

I hope to see you soon and we can reminisce and weep together for a life well lived.

With much love and hugs,

X

Genesis 50.1-2, 10 And Joseph fell upon his father's face, and wept upon him, and kissed him. And Joseph commanded his servants the physicians to embalm his father: and the physicians embalmed Israel. And they came to the threshing floor of A-tad, which is beyond Jordan, and there they mourned with a great and very sore lamentation: and he made a mourning for his father seven days.

Exodus 20.12; Isaiah 41.10; St. Matthew 25.21; St. John 11.25-26; St. John 14.26; 2 Corinthians 1.3-4; 1 Thessalonians 4.14; 1 Timothy 4.12b; Revelation 21.4.

Death of a Sibling

Oh my dear, I am so very, very sorry for your loss. You will be gutted. Your dear brother meant so much to you. He was always there for you and fought your corner with your parents when need be. You were a godly example of a brother and sister living together in unity. You will feel as if your right arm has been cut off. He was that important to you. You did not go around saying 'I love you' 'cos that is just not how your family relates to one another. But he knew that you loved him by all the many acts of love that you demonstrated to him and he loved you in return.

There is something about the death of a sibling that is different from that of a parent or friend. You have gone through life with a sibling. There is shared history that is unique to the two of you: family 'in' jokes and phrases; memories of times past; quirky humorous phrases that only have a special meaning between you both. The eye rolling at certain family events where only you both know, and can read, the body language. While others may share in the stories, they do not necessarily share the experience that is yours, and yours alone. Your own past history is being reduced to memories as opposed to a shared, lived experience.

The death of a sibling also implies that death has now hit our own generation and is a reminder of our own mortality. There is an expected natural order of things, although we all know that this is not, in fact, reality. Parents die first, siblings, then the next generation. We both know this is not what happens in practice but these things are out-with our control.

We thank God for your brother. You shared your childhood and teenage years with a wonderful guy. As adults, leading independent lives, you still had that deep bond of love that meant you were there for each other while still living your own lives.

I too have my happy memories that will take many cups of coffee to chat over. Do you remember how he used to rugby tackle us as we walked through the hall? Then when he passed his driving test that opened up a whole new world for us, as it meant we could go to the youth fellowship on a Sunday night and get a lift home. We thought we were so grown up joining the YF.

I pray that happier memories bring you peace. I hope you will find time to reflect on your lives together. Maybe you would consider writing a journal of some of your memories to keep these alive as a memento of him?

Celebrate the life he had. Celebrate the wonderful man that he was. Thank God for your brother's life, witness and example. And when you are in the depths of sorrow, be thankful that you knew him and that as he played a huge part in your life, so you also played a large, enhancing part in his life.

With my love, prayers and virtual hugs,

X

Hebrews 13.1 Let brotherly love continue.

Genesis 43.30; Psalm 133.1; St. John 1.40-42; Ephesians 5.1-2; Philippians 3.17; 1 Timothy 4.12b; Philemon 7; James 2.14; 1 John 4.20-21.

Facing Death

O my dear friend

I am writing this while you are alive as there is no point in writing it when you are not.

I am writing this with tears streaming down my face. I can't believe it – but you can. I cannot believe that your time on this earth is now severely limited and our time together limited even more so. I can't believe that you are going to heaven before me.

In some ways you are privileged to know that your time on earth is coming to an end. No more worries about the bills, the house and all the other daily chores that seem so important at the time but are rather just things that keep us going. You have time to prepare and to put what you can in order. You have some time to say your goodbyes to friends and families.

I am writing to thank you for your friendship over many, many years. We have shared so much, laughter and tears, concerns about our families, concerns about our Church and friends and worldwide situations. We have stood by each other through thick and thin. We have prayed together, worshipped together. We have enjoyed the communion of saints. All these memories are tinged with the poignancy of knowing that you go before to the prepared place.

When you get there, will you please say hello to all our friends and family who are already there? Will you look out for them and tell them that they are never forgotten?

In some ways I am jealous of you. You will get to see our Lord soon. You will soon be at rest from your earthly travails.

But O how much I will grieve you. Grief is such a selfish emotion as it is all about what I have lost and yet, I take comfort in the fact that our Lord grieved his friend Lazarus. He has promised to comfort all those who mourn so He knows what I feel.

In the remaining days, please enjoy the time with your family and those closest to you. Reserve your energies for what really matters and do not waste them on fruitless conversations. Take comfort from knowing that the Lord is near you. He is beside you, within you, above you, beneath you. Every breath you take is from Him and when you no longer need that breath, you will be asleep with Him. What more could we all want?

For to me to live *is* Christ, and to die *is* gain.

Goodbye, dear friend. Until we meet again in heaven, God hold us all in the hollow of His hand.

With all my love,

Your sister in Christ,

Amen.

X

Isaiah 41.13-14 For I the Lord thy God will hold thy right hand, saying unto thee, Fear not; I will help thee. Fear not, thou worm Jacob, *and* ye men of Israel; I will help thee, saith the Lord, and thy redeemer, the Holy One of Israel.

Psalm 34.18; St. Matthew 5.4; St. John 11.35; St. John 14.1-4; Philippians 1.21; 1 Thessalonians 4.13-14; Titus 3.9; Hebrews 4.15-16; Revelation 21.4.

Work

Choosing a Career

Hi my dear, Are we not so very, very fortunate in this day and age that life-long learning is accepted, embraced and desired? I am not suggesting that your choice of career is not important, all I am saying is that we are fortunate because if we find that we are not in the right place, it is possible to change our course and direction.

Some people even say that, in this day and age, people can expect to have three career changes in their working life. I have seen this is some people – but not in everyone.

Given all the above, does your choice of career matter and how do you make your choice?

I am not sure that it is always clear cut. Certainly your current qualifications will open some doors to you and your lack of others will shut some for you. That is life and that is only right.

Ask advice from people who know you about the kind of work that they think you would enjoy. Listen carefully to how people respond. Don't jump into their reply and say 'No', rather write down all their suggestions and in the privacy of your own room, prayerfully consider each and every option.

Is there something that you would love to do? Is it a passion for you and you know that this is what you were 'made' for? If so, find out all you can about that job or career. What do you need to get to position yourself to do that job? Do you need further studying? Do you need to learn a new skill?

Are there jobs in that area or is it something that you love to do, but know that there is no sustainable, paid, employment in that area and so this needs to be a hobby at the moment?

What is your gifting and enabling? Not many people know their own strengths, weaknesses and so again, asking advice of others is important. Again, take any comments and consider them quietly. Don't be offended at what some people might say. They see one side of you and what they might say (that you construe as negative) others can see as a positive attribute.

Throughout it all, bring your heart before God. He made you. He has gifted and enabled you. Some people have a very specific calling and others God has given special talents. Look at the people in the Bible with various gifts and enabling. While these are not definitive talents, they do show us that put at God's disposal, He can use us wherever He chooses.

The Lord has promised to guide us and to lead us. Sometimes our sin and pride can stop us seeing His ways. So make sure that you regularly bring your sins before Him and ask for His cleansing, forgiveness and restoration. If we put our ALL at His disposal, He will make the way plain for us. We cannot hold anything back but trust that He knows what is best for us.

I have found that, sometimes, the Lord does not make the way clear until we are willing to follow Him, regardless of the cost and where-ever He may lead. This is hard for some people to take but we have examples in our Bible. Abraham did not know where he was going but he set out in faith that the Lord would guide him. So, if your heart is right with God, He will show you the way.

Thereafter, start applying for jobs, for studying, for courses. He will show you the way and He will grant you that peace that passes all understanding. There is nothing better than being at the centre of God's will. It does not mean that it will be easy. Not at all. It does mean that you have His power, through the Holy Spirit, to enable you to do what He plans for you.

We all claim that we want to know Jesus more. Really? As I read it in my Bible, to know Jesus means we have to know Him in His suffering. Are we really saying we want to suffer? When we read our Bibles, we see that most of the Godly leaders grew during times of suffering and not so much in times of plenty. So, if your career, or job, is hard going, this should drive you to seek the Lord more and not the opposite. There are times when there are things which are unacceptable at work e.g. sexual harassment, but a hard job, on its own, does not mean that you are in the wrong job. Instead, ask God what you are to learn in this hard time and how you are meant to show Him to those around you.

Discerning the will of the Lord is an exciting time. It may defy human logic. It will stretch you, but, as we make it our goal to please Him, so He takes and uses our frail offerings, all for His praise and glory.

You know I am happy to continue talking these things through with you and am prayerfully considering how the Lord is leading you. To Him be all the praise and glory.

Blessings and love,

X

Isaiah 58.11 And the Lord shall guide thee continually, and satisfy thy soul in drought, and make fat thy bones: and thou shalt be like a watered garden, and like a spring of water, whose waters fail not.

Genesis 12.1; Exodus 35.31-33; 2 Chronicles 2.7; Nehemiah 3.3, 8;.31a; Nehemiah 7.1-2; Psalm 16.11; Psalm 32.8; Isaiah 6.8; Isaiah 30.21; St. Luke 9.62; 1 Corinthians 7.7; 2 Corinthians 5.9; Philippians 3. 10-11; Philippians 4.7, 13; Hebrews 13.5; 1 Peter 5.7; 1 John 1.9; 1 John 5.14-15.

Redundancy

Hi pal, I was so very, very sorry to hear that you have lost your job. I know how committed you were to it. I know you gave over and above, well beyond the call of duty. I know you will be gutted.

You will feel worthless. You will feel bereft. You will be angry that others, perhaps less able than you, have retained their jobs and yet you have been let go. You will be angry at your boss, at management and, perhaps, angry at God. God can cope with your anger. It is right to vent your spleen and let your anger out.

God tells us not to let the sun go down on our wrath. It is good to let it all out and to scream, cry and such things. Please just do not break that beautiful vase that you have in your sitting room! That achieves nothing.

You know that your self-worth is not dependent on your work. The Lord has made you. You are His unique, wonderful creation. He has made you. He is the potter and we are the clay. He is moulding and shaping you in accordance with His will to be His salt and light in this world. He loves you so much that He sent His only Son to die on the cross for your sins. Your self-worth does not come from your job. Your self-worth comes from how our Lord sees you: He loves you, He made you in His image, He died to save you. None of that can be taken away from you, regardless of your job.

You know that your abilities will be needed and wanted by someone else. If you put yourself into the Lord's hands, He will use you to fulfil His purposes. He has given us a picture of the body where every organ has a part to play. So, find comfort first and foremost in your Church. Tell your friends in Church what has happened and ask them to pray for you and to support you during these hard days. You are hurting, so the whole body will hurt with you. Keep an open mind about job opportunities. Perhaps the Lord wants to place you somewhere else in this world. Please not, as I selfishly enjoy your company!!! Perhaps the Lord wants to lead you in a different direction. Strive to find the narrow way – that leads to life and not to destruction.

You know that our Lord, who supplies your every need, will provide for you. It may take time. It may take retraining. It may mean a salary cut. However, do you not think that He knew this was coming? He knows what lies ahead. He knows the way that you will take. He is ahead of you.

In the meantime, this is an opportunity to stop your routines and to reflect, pray and consider what God has planned for you. Does He want to move you in a different direction? Is He prompting you to take up a hobby? Does He want you to be quiet and spend more time with Him? Is He calling you aside to hear Him better and more? What do you think the Lord is saying to you in all this?

You are angry just now and I totally understand that. In the fullness of time, your anger will recede and I pray that you will see this as the push that you needed to go somewhere different, to try something else, to experience the gracious loving hands of the Lord shaping you into His precious vessel.

In the meantime, get your diary out. How are you placed for a coffee and a proper chat next week? There is a brilliant new coffee shop near me and I thought we could try it out. I am standing with you in this experience. The Lord will see you through.

With much love,

Your dear friend,

X

Isaiah 29.16 Surely your turning of things upside down shall be esteemed as the potter's clay: for shall the work say of him that made it, He made me not? or shall the thing framed say of him that framed it, He had no understanding?

Deuteronomy 31.8; 1 Kings 19.12; Job 23.10; Psalm 35.17; Psalm 119.73; Isaiah 64.8; Habakkuk 1.2; St. Matthew 5.13-14; St. Matthew 7.13-14; Romans 12.1-2,15; 1 Corinthians 7.7; 1 Corinthians 12.12; Ephesians 4.26-27; Ephesians 6.7-8; Philippians 4.19; 1 Timothy 1.15; 1 Peter 2.9; 1 Peter 3.18.

Change at Work

Hi dear, thank you for opening up to me about the changes in your work. I know that change is not easy and yet, all around us nature changes: daily, monthly, and seasonally. We change as we grow older (and fatter!!) and we love to see our children and grandchildren grow. There would be something wrong if they did not grow. The Bible tells us that Jesus grew in spirit and truth and that Samuel also grew in his knowledge of the Lord.

So, we are surrounded by change on a daily basis. Nothing stays the same except for Jesus. Change is part of this world. In the past, when I have been faced with change I have sometimes made a list: what parts of the change do I like? What parts do I dislike? What strengths, weaknesses, opportunities and threats are there in this change? Maybe not a Biblical concept but well worth considering. If you were to do this, you might actually see that there are some parts of this change that you actually like. Maybe you can get rid of some parts of your job that you no longer like? Maybe there is an opportunity to learn a new skill in one particular area that has been denied you up until now?

Through it all, your attitude is so important. Remember that our Lord gave up everything for us and His attitude was that of a servant. Remember that your earthly Masters are initiating this change but we serve a greater Master and we are encouraged to do all that we do as if serving our Lord, and not another human being. Remember that everyone else is changing around you as well. There will be moans and gossip. Try not to participate in these as it is not honouring to your earthly masters nor does such conversation edify others.

If you think there are specific aspects that will not work, then graciously mention these to your boss. Wait until you have made a list and don't hassle your boss with small insignificant details. Somethings are outwith our control within the work environment and sometimes we just need to embrace the change, go with the flow and see how it all works out.

Through it all, our Lord knows where you are. He has placed you in your workplace. He wants you to be His salt and light in this situation. Trust Him to speak through you to others: words of encouragement and affirmation; words of wise counsel; words that build up others and do not destroy them. Before you know it, this change will be the new norm and you will wonder what all the fuss was about....until the next change happens.

I look forward to hearing more about it when I see you next week.

With much love,

X

Colossians 3.23 And whatsoever ye do, do *it* heartedly, as to the Lord, and not unto men;

Genesis 8.22; 1 Samuel 2.26; Psalm 37.23-24; St. Matthew 5.13-14; St. Luke 2.52; St. Luke 14.28; Ephesians 4. 29;

Ephesians 6.7-8; Philippians 2.5-8, 14-15; 2 Timothy 2.23-24; Hebrews 13.8; James 1.5.

Not Getting that Job

Dear friend,

I know many people will quote Jeremiah 29.11 at you:

'For I know the thoughts that I think towards you, saith the Lord, thoughts of peace, and not of evil, to give you an expected end' and I know that inside you will go – fine! After all, those verses were given to a people in exile and for a whole population and yet we quote them for individuals.

I know many people will quote Proverbs 3.5-6 at you:

'Trust in the Lord with all thine heart; and lean not unto thine own understanding. In all thy ways acknowledge him, and he shall direct thy paths', and there will be the silent implicit word that you are going the wrong way and have not trusted God enough.

Let's just accept that God loves you. God's heart is to give you life in all its fullness. He knows what this job would have meant to you: possibly promotion, possibly more money, possibly more influence and authority. He knows how you would have liked and handled the more disposable income, the status and influence and the positive impact on others. He knows the resulting pressure and pride and its impact on you as a person, on your family and friends. So perhaps, the Lord has spared you from yourself? Perhaps He has said that while this looks good, and it is not wrong in itself, it is not right for you; for you, the person that He has made you to be. He knows that you are dust. He knows your gifting and enabling as He made you as the potter makes pots with the clay.

I know it hurts but there is a bigger picture here. You do not know what is just round the corner and you may be expected to stand up and take greater responsibility in another part of your life. You would not be able to do that if you had this job. You do not know how He is forming you and shaping you through this disappointment (if you let Him) to make you more like His Son, Jesus. You do not know what else He wants to give you, do through you and, this job would be a distraction.

Yes, you went for the job with all faith and all hope and all purpose. But the Lord has also said that His thoughts are not our thoughts and His ways are not our ways.

Trust Him to fulfil His purposes through you. Trust Him to provide for all your needs as He has said He would do. Trust Him, as your loving heavenly Father, who cares for His children. Trust Him – not yourself, not a job, not your own means -only Him who is your creator, redeemer and friend.

Your dear friend in Christ,

X

Romans 9.20-21 Nay but, O man, who art thou that repliest against God? Shall the thing formed say to him that formed *it,* Why hast thou made me thus? Hath not the potter power over the clay, of the same lump to make one vessel unto honour, and another unto dishonour?

Genesis 2.7; Exodus 13.17; 1 Samuel 24.10; Psalm 37.5; Proverbs 3.5-6; Isaiah 55.9; Jeremiah 17.7; Jeremiah 29.11; St. John 10.10; St. John 14.1; 2 Corinthians 3.18; 2 Corinthians 5.9; Philippians 4.12-13; 1 Thessalonians 4.11; 2 Peter 2.4-5,9;

Themes

Waiting

Friend, what can I say? I have heard that you are waiting on that result before you do anything. Why are you waiting and, what are you waiting for? Waiting is not wasting time. Wasting time is wasting time. Waiting is an active word so how do you wait, what are you waiting for and how are you preparing yourself for when the result is known?

Think of flower bulbs. We plant them in the ground months before we see the green shoots rising through the earth. They are not doing nothing while they are in the ground. They are waiting for the sun and the right conditions for them to grow. They are absorbing nutrients and moisture from the earth. They are preparing themselves for the right time. We cannot see a lot of that, but it is happening.

You want to be married. So how are you preparing yourself to be a wife? How are you building a home where you are? What healthy habits are you currently adopting? Can you cook? Do you clean? Do you live in a house, a hovel or a home? Pray about what is needed to build a godly home and, by God's grace, start working towards that.

You want to have children. Of course you do. So how are you preparing yourself to be a mother? Do you like children? Are you currently working with children? Do you know what is important for child development? Are you investing in any children at the moment so that, in case you are not able to have children, you are still involved in the lives of others' children? Just remember, children are not a 'right' and we are told that 'more are the children of those who do not have any than of those who do have them'.

So, how are you waiting: excitedly, nervously, patiently, hopefully, fruitfully? God prepares us in the waiting for what His plans and purposes are for us. Are you waiting in tune with Him so that, when His purposes are revealed, you can willingly accept and embrace them?

We are encouraged so often to wait on the Lord. Wait for Him. Not wait to hear about Him; wait to read about Him; wait to talk about Him. Wait for Him – the person of the Lord Jesus Christ, revealed to us by His Spirit. This kind of waiting is quiet and peaceful, it is full of hope and love, it is a blessed assurance that He is with us always.

I pray for you as you wait for that result. I pray that God is preparing you for the next stage in your life, whatever that might be. I pray that His presence and peace pervade your whole being so that, like Mary, you are able to say 'Behold the handmaid of the Lord. Be it unto me as you will.'

Your dear friend,

X

Psalm 130.5 I wait for the Lord, my soul doth wait, and in his word do I hope.

Exodus 33.14; Esther 4.14; Psalm 25.5; Psalm 27.14; Psalm 37.7; Psalm 40.1; Proverbs 20.22; Proverbs 24.3-4; Lamentations 3. 22–26; Isaiah 30.18; Isaiah 54.1; Daniel 10.12-13; Micah 7.7; St. Matthew 25.10-13; St. Matthew

28.19-20; St. Luke 1.38; Romans 8.24-25; Colossians 1.10-12; James 5.7-8; 2 Peter 3.9.

Pain

As the deer pants for the water, so my soul longs after you, the living God. The sea roars and the moon commands the tides and the waters. In the storm, the gathering waves pound the shore and the rocks, cliffs and caves. The dark, frothy waters crash onto the beach relentlessly, time after time. The moonlight does not alter the beating of the shores as wave after wave powerfully drops its white horses onto the sandy shoreline.

Meeting the cliff face, the waters crash and pound and spray into the air before descending like flowing hair back onto itself. The flumes of the sea dance in the forces of nature as its onward force meets the obstruction that causes it to stop. The shingle on the shore clatters and chatters as the small, colourful stones are pulled back into the ravaging sea with each tidal wave.

In the quiet of the daytime, the lapping waters brush and tickle the sea edges between the turquoise green sea and the soft, sandy beach. The waters still come in quietness and strength but they bring a calming presence and a peaceful perspective of the deep, roaring seas. The ebb and flow of the tide is timely, purposeful, gentle and needed.

So your pain ravages your body, my dear friend. Sometimes it is relentless, all consuming, and drives all other thoughts from your mind. Other times it is quieter, still there, but not quite so bad. It is a timely reminder that you are still alive. Yet through it all, our Lord knows what you are going through. Through it all, He is there with you.

The Lord has given others the knowledge and skills to know what medications will help your pain. He has skilled others in alternative medicines and other forms of diverse therapies to help you cope. Use them all. This pain may be for a season. Let Him minister to you through others and through various means. He is the Lord. He knows our end from the beginning. He knows what you can bear and when He has tried you, you will come forth as gold. Hold on dear friend, it is our Father's will to give you His kingdom. Use all means to control this pain and trust God to fulfil His purposes in and through you.

By cool Siloam's shady rill – may you soon reach that place of peace, of surrender and shade where healing has happened and you can rest up in His love again and bask in His glory and presence. To God alone be all the glory.

The Lord has promised to guide you and lead you in the way you should go. Trust Him to do this. Wait and see what He has planned for you, dear friend.

I look forward to hearing more about His working in your life.

With my love,

X

Hebrews 13.5b-6 for he hath said, I will never leave thee, nor forsake thee. So that we may boldly say, The Lord *is* my helper, and I will not fear what man shall do unto me.

1 Samuel 12.16; Job 23.10; Psalm 32.8; Psalm 42.1; Psalm 138.8; Ecclesiastes 3.1; Isaiah 26.3-4; Isaiah 30.15b; Isaiah 53.4-5; St. Mark 4.39; St. Luke 12.32; St. Luke 19.40; 2 Corinthians 12.9; 1 Timothy 1.17; Jude 24-25; Revelation 21.4.

Be Still

Be still.

Just be still.

Your heavenly Father knows what you need before you even ask Him.

So be still.

Enjoy being

In His presence.

Enjoy listening

To His voice.

His affirmation on your life.

You are a royal priesthood.

A holy nation.

To declare His purposes over this earth.

Enjoy His laughter

Over all the crazy things we do.

Enjoy His gentle, reprimand

Over all the crazy things we do!

Be still.

The voice of the Lord is heard

In the stillness.

Be still

For He is God.

Be still.

Rest in His presence.

Draw deeply from Him

The living Water

The Bread of life.

He carries our burdens

He knows our frame

He remembers that we are dust.

Be still. The Lord is near.

Zephaniah 1.7a Hold thy peace at the presence of the lord God: for the day of the Lord *is* at hand:

Exodus 14.13 ; Numbers 16.5b; 1 Kings 19.12; Job 37.14; Psalm 2.4; Psalm 46.10; Psalm 103.14; Psalm 145.18; Lamentations 3, 27,28; St. Matthew 6.32b; St. John 6.35; St. John 13.23; Hebrews 12.6; 1 Peter 2.5.

Hoping

Och aye, I meant to say to you, that I know you are hoping to go to university, but if that does not happen, you know it is not the end of the world? God is working His purposes out.

People hope for more money, a better life, the sun (!) and all the rest. But what is hope? Is it not wishful thinking? Can we think or will anything into being –of course we cannot. Can't you see that you are hoping for things – over which you have no control: good weather, happy lives, health?

The Bible tells us that we should hope in God and only in Him, because He is the God of hope. He knows what we need. He knows our frame. He remembers that we are dust. He has promised to never leave us. He has promised to supply all our needs in Christ Jesus. He hears our prayers and answers them. His promises never fail, they are new every morning.

We are told not to hope in other situations as they cannot supply what we need. We might think that they can–and our Lord can use people to fulfil His purposes but, in the end, it is only the Lord who provides.

As the psalmists says 'Hope thou in God: for I shall yet praise him.' So hope in God, hope in His word, hope in His love, hope in our Saviour – our sure and certain hope in troubled times. Through hoping in Him, we can know a peace and a joy that surpasses all understanding – regardless of our circumstances and situation.

So, hopefully (no pun intended!), the next time someone asks you what your plans are, I wonder how you will answer them? I do admit that I am praying that you get into university I think you are able and I think the course you are thinking of studying would suit you. However, I entrust you into the loving care of our heavenly Father, who knows, far better than me, what is best for you!

With much love,

Your pal,

X

Romans 15.13 Now the God of hope fill you with all joy and peace in believing, that ye may abound in hope, through the power of the Holy Ghost.

Deuteronomy 31.6; Psalm 20.7; Psalm 33.18; Psalm 43.5; Psalm 103.14; Psalm 147.11; Proverbs 23.18; Isaiah 40.31; Jeremiah 33.3; Lamentations 3. 22-26; Micah 7.7; St. Luke 12.25; Romans 8. 24-25; Romans 15.4; 2 Corinthians 4.18; Ephesians 1.18; Philippians 4.7, 12-13, 19; 1 Thessalonians 1.3; 1 Timothy 4.10; Hebrews 6.19; Hebrews 10.23; 1 Peter 1.13.

Directions in Life

Hi there, thank you so much for your email and for sharing your angst about which direction to take at the moment. If only someone would tell us what we should do and where we should go, that would be fine, wouldn't it? I suppose we are all looking for directions in life and at every stage in life, our direction may change and alter.

Do we listen to that inner voice, the one that tells us not to heed the right or the left but to keep on going? Or do we explore different options, weighing up the pros and cons for each? So often, directions do not come in flashes of blue lightening but rather in various ways and means.

Pray over any decisions that you need to make. Commit it all to God and He will show you the way that you should go. Be prepared to follow Him, before He shows you the way, then you will go in His light and strength and not your own. So often, directions are between good, better and best and not between bad and good – is that not true? Discerning the truth among the lies and the appearances can be hard but remember that the Lord looks at the heart and not the outward appearance. Keep focused on Him. There is a place for asking for a specific sign and setting out a fleece. There is also a place for casting lots. God will work in all mysterious ways to reveal His plans and purposes to us, if we are willing to follow Him.

Read His word. Know Him – in His suffering and His death. Read what He sets His heart upon. Read what makes Him angry and what He loves. Remember that His word is quick and active and sharper than any two edged sword. Every time you open it, you are holding a stick of dynamite in your hands. His word speaks right into your heart and mind and will guide you and lead you in the way you should go.

Ask a few trusted friends to pray with you and for you. I hope you would consider me one such friend. Listen to their wisdom. You do not need to act on it, but listen to what they say and bring that before the Lord as well. Remember Job's comforters. Also remember the saints who care passionately for the work of God and for your part in that. So, ask for wisdom to discern what friends are saying in the light of God's word and in the revelation that you think God is giving you.

Weigh up the impact of this direction on you, your family, your friends and your Church. The Lord wants our all, nothing more and nothing less. He wants disciples, not half hearted followers. He wants the best as He showed us in the Garden of Eden. Explore what is required of each option available to you. Let the Lord guide your footsteps.

Pray again-you are getting the message here aren't you? His Holy Spirit will lead you into the right way.

Then go for it! Our Lord is gracious. He will guide your steps. The Lord is our Shepherd, we shall not want. What a wonderful statement and promise.

Tons of love,

X

Romans 12.1-2 I beseech you therefore, brethren, by the mercies of God, that ye present your bodies a living sacrifice, holy, acceptable unto God, *which is* your reasonable service. And be not conformed to this world: but be ye transformed by the renewing of your mind, that ye may prove what *is* that good, and acceptable and perfect, will of God.

Genesis 1.31; Judges 6. 17; 1 Samuel 16.7; Psalm 23.1; Psalm 37.5; Psalm 119.105; Proverbs 6.6; Proverbs 16.3; Isaiah 30.21; Micah 6.8; St. Matthew 10.37-39; St. Matthew 28.19-20; St. John 16.13; Acts 1.26; Philippians 3. 10-11; Hebrews 4.12; Revelation 1.16.

Walking

Thank you so much for that wonderful walk we had today. I thoroughly enjoyed your company, our fellowship, the time together and not forgetting the fantastic cake and coffee in that shop. We definitely must repeat that whole exercise soon.

I was reflecting on our chat and on the many walks that people had in the Bible. I thought on the 40 years that the children of Israel spent going through the desert. Do you remember the time when we were praying for that new job for you and it seemed to be ages before the door opened? How many times did we pound round the park, pushing our children in their buggies while agonising over that problem?

Then there was the time when your son got into university. Oh that was just such brilliant news for us all! I could hear your shrieks even before I opened the door. I never actually told you this, but I heard your footsteps pounding up the drive, way before I heard your voice. I knew it had to be something special with the speed at which you were running. Your face told it all! I saw the joy, the pride, the pleasure and the hopes and anticipation for his future. All celebrated in due course but I will never forget your face when you brought such good news.

Then there was the time when we walked by the local canal. You had just dropped your son off at his halls of residence with his bags of clothes; the carrier bags of food; his guitar (of course) and you told me how he would not let you hug or kiss him as he said goodbye. A hard time for you but, as we walked, you were also very proud that he had made the break from home and was now standing on his own two feet.

Do you recall the time when I was at my wits end at work? We took a drive to the seashore and as I paddled in the waves and vented my spleen, again, you suddenly stopped, put your hands on my shoulders and prayed for the whole situation. I will never forget the holy peace that descended and calmed my mind and heart. My feet were freezing but the rest of me glowed inside with a Godly warmth.

We have been friends for how long now? It must be approaching 20 years at least. I suppose in many ways we have 'walked' together through happy and sad times; challenging and peaceful times; struggling and not quite so struggling times. Throughout it all though, I know that you have listened when I have gone on... and on.... and on... and afterwards, I know that you have taken all my worries to God on my behalf. I hope you know that I too have lifted you, your family and concerns before the Lord as well.

I am just so thankful for our friendship and fellowship and, continue to be, as we walk through life together. Thank you my dear friend for being there.

With love,

X

Luke 24.13-16 And, behold, two of them went that same day to a village called Emmaus, which was from Jerusalem *about* threescore furlongs. And they talked together of all these things which had happened. And it came to pass, that, while they communed *together* and reasoned, Jesus himself drew near, and went with them. But their eyes were holden that they should not know him.

Joshua 5.6a; 1 Samuel 1.24, 28; Ecclesiastes 4.12; St. Matthew 18.20; St. John 20. 1-2; 2 Corinthians 5.7; Philippians 1.3; Philippians 4.7; 1 Thessalonians 1.2-3.

A Blessing

Dear friend

May the Lord bless you and keep you

May the Lord grant you His presence as you journey through this life

May you know His peace in your heart and mind

May you be blessed by Him as you walk each day beside Him

May you know His strength to face the difficult conversations that you may have

May you know His joy when you see Him working in your life and the life of others

May you know the fulfilment of living a life in His service

I look forward to seeing you in heaven.

Until then,

God bless you.

X

Printed in Great Britain
by Amazon

35049685R10059